The courage to be me

A story of courage, self-compassion and hope after sexual abuse.

By Dr Nina Burrowes

Published by NB Research Ltd,
First Floor, 80 Haymarket,
London, SW1Y 4TE

Cover illustration by Katie Green.

Illustrated by

Alexander Bertram-Powell
Nina Burrowes
Katie Green
Jade Sarson
and
Heather Wilson

The courage to be me

A story of courage, self-compassion and hope after sexual abuse.

By Dr Nina Burrowes

Hello. I'm Nina.
I'd like to tell you a story

It's a story that doesn't normally get told.

A story about life after rape or sexual abuse.

We don't tell enough stories about abuse.

This silence means that many people
who have been abused live with
it in isolation.

Before you start the book there are some things that you may want to know.

There are no images of actual rape or sexual abuse in this book.

This book may not reflect your story. There are millions of stories of life after abuse, this book only has room to tell five. If the book doesn't reflect your experience that isn't because what happened to you is weird or unusual - the book is just too small to cover everything.

The book only tells the story of *beginning* to rebuild your life after abuse. Life after abuse *can* be wonderful - but it's a long journey. There are no easy solutions in this book. Sadly, there aren't any.

There are no images of actual
rape or sexual abuse in this book.

This book may not reflect your story.
There are millions of stories of life
after abuse, this book only has
room to tell five. If the book doesn't
reflect your experience that isn't
because what happened to you
is weird or unusual - the book is
just too small to cover everything.

The book only tells the story of
beginning to rebuild your life after
abuse. Life after abuse *can* be
wonderful - but it's a long journey.
There are no easy solutions
in this book. Sadly, there aren't any.

My intention has been to tell a powerful and ultimately beautiful human story.

But if you have experienced rape or sexual abuse in the past you may find reading this book difficult.

Nina's tips for looking after yourself
when you're reading this book:

Make sure *now* is a good time for you
to read this book.

Think about where and when you read
this book. Choose a space that feels
safe and a time that feels right.

Take your time when you're reading this
book. Read it in chunks and take breaks.

To help remind you to look after yourself this book has some cats.

The cats appear throughout the book.

When you see a cat it's a reminder to take a break if you need it.

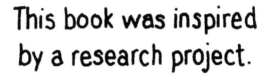

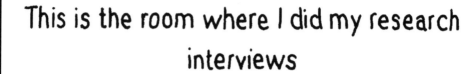

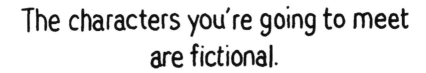

The characters you're going to meet are fictional.

But their stories reflect the experiences of millions of women, men, boys, and girls around the world.

The people I've met who've had the
courage to rebuild their lives after abuse
are inspirational

The courage to be me

A story of courage, self-compassion and hope
after sexual abuse.

By Dr Nina Burrowes

I hope this book inspires
you in the same way they
inspire me

Table of contents

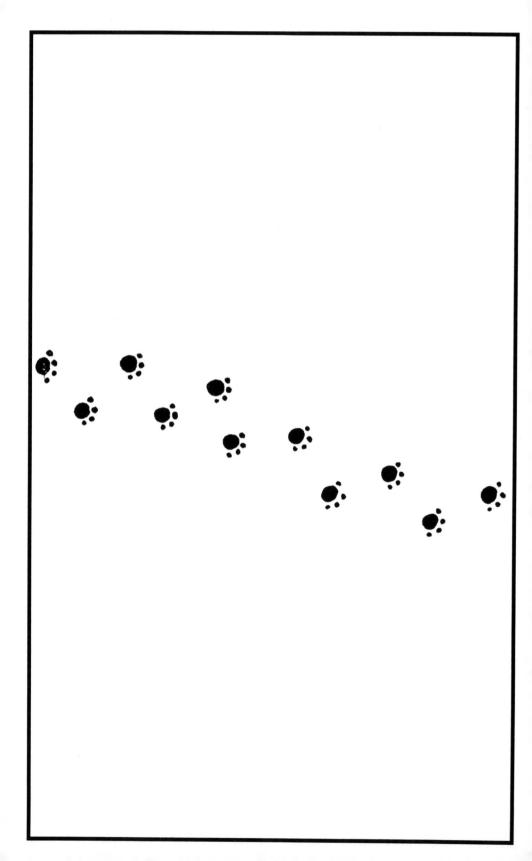

Chapter 1
Do I belong here?

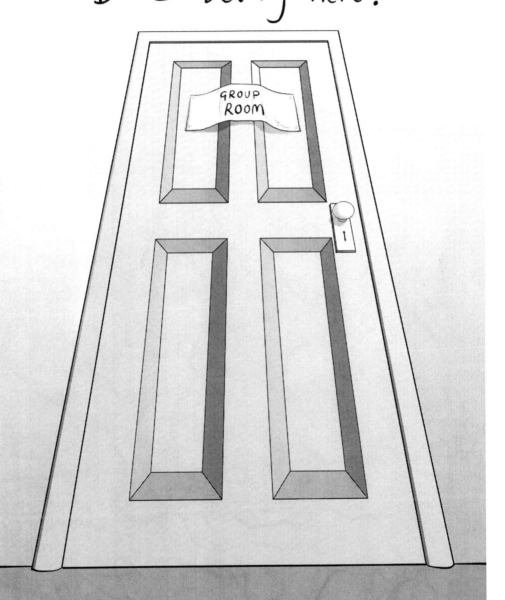

I had developed a way of
being somewhere
and yet
not
being
there.

I could be in a room full of people, with life all around me...

There could be laughter...

...tears...

...arguments...

It's like I'm in a double glazed box.

I can see and hear things, but they are in the distance...

I'm disconnected.

I spent most of the first session staring at my feet.

Exploring the Pattern in the Carpet.

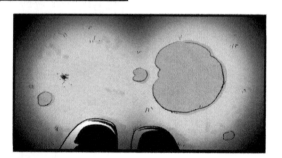

Looking at the stitching on my shoes,

looking but not seeing.

It was my way of being there.

And yet not being there.

It made my world feel safe.

Safe, but small.

We'd all experienced something that had turned us into experts at *coping*.

All of us were doing what we could to make ourselves feel safe. But all of us were there because we didn't feel safe at all.

Although I couldn't tell you much more about that first session, it's actually the session I'm *most proud of.*

Because I was **there.**

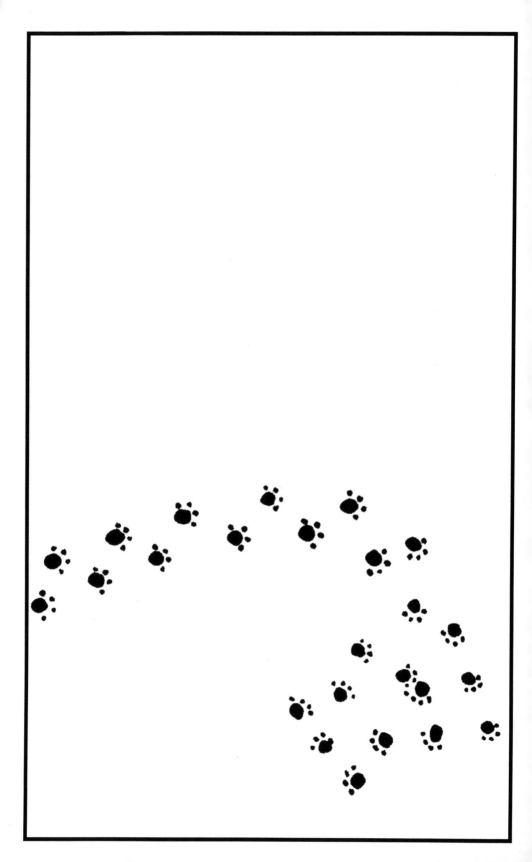

Chapter 2
I'm *not* mad?

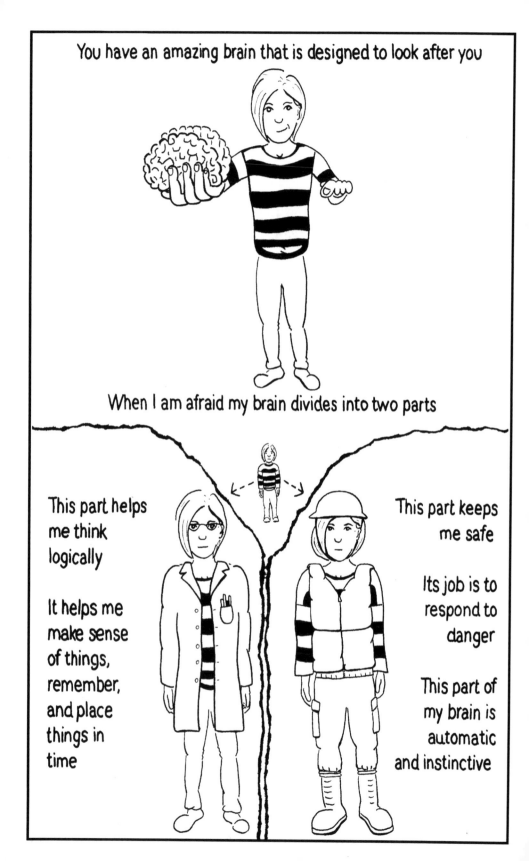

When I detect danger my instinctive brain takes over

This makes sense. I need to act fast and survive. *Then* I can think about it.

My brain enters danger mode
It is getting ready to respond in one of three ways

FIGHT   FLIGHT   FREEZE

My brain selects the tactic that is most likely to keep me alive.

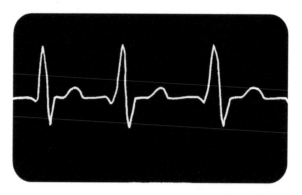

It's not interested in how I will feel afterwards
or what other people will think.

THIS IS LIFE AND DEATH

I'm likely to freeze

My instinctive brain knows that as a human being
I am weaker and slower than my natural predators

I'm even less likely to fight or run away from someone I trust

My instinctive brain knows that my survival has always depended on the love and care of others

I want to run *towards* the people I trust when I am frightened

So whilst my logical brain might think

I should fight

I should scream

I should run

My instinctive brain is in control of my body

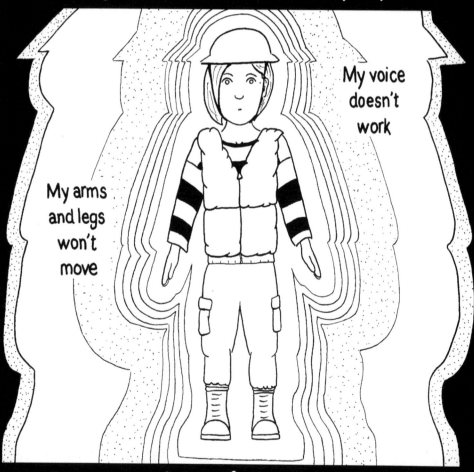

My voice doesn't work

My arms and legs won't move

I am frozen

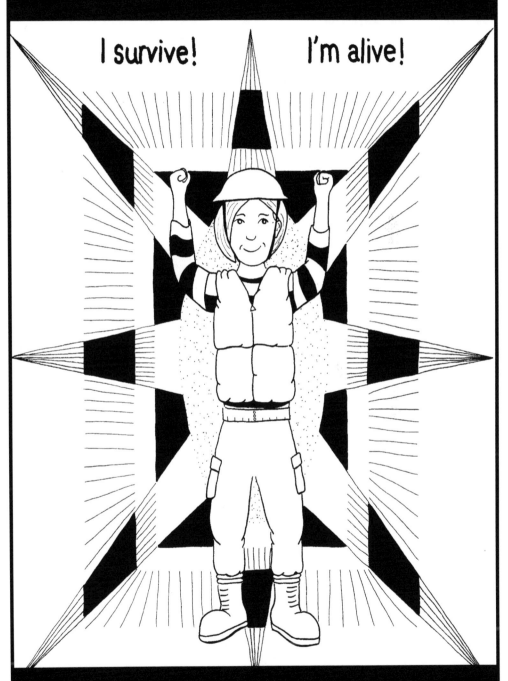

When this happens I feel like I am always surrounded by danger

DANGER

I am constantly vigilant. I look for danger everywhere.

This can become a cycle. Because I am unable to make sense of what happened to me and assign it to the past no matter how far I travel...

I can end up reliving how I felt in that moment again...

...and again.

Although the abuse may have happened a long time ago it can create a ripple effect that runs through you.

Living with the impact of abuse can become *harder* over time.

My brain has changed and this is just going to get harder? So I *am* mad?

You're not mad. All of this time your brain has been doing what it's designed to do. It's trying to look after you. But it's got stuck and it needs some help.

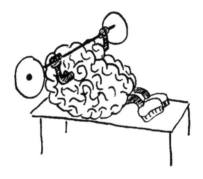

Your brain is like a muscle

With help and hard work you can change it

Let me show you...

The thing I struggle with the most is my sense of guilt. I feel responsible for the abuse. Is that my brain looking after me too?

Many people who've experienced rape or sexual abuse have feelings of guilt. It can be one of the hardest parts of living with abuse.

And it can also be an example of your mind trying to look after you.

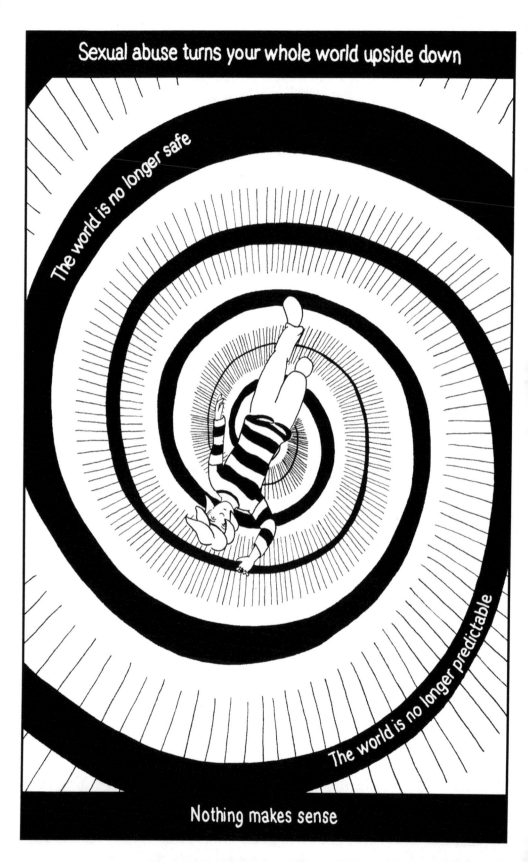

Guilt can be a way of taking control again

Blaming yourself for what you did or did not do feels bad but it's a way of making yourself feel safe and in control.

Saying...

It was my fault.

... is a way of saying 'I can stop it from happening again'.

Guilt is also a way of protecting your relationship with your abuser. Most people are abused by someone they trust.

Guilt helps to explain the unexplainable

The guilt also helps you to stay in a relationship that you may not be ready or able to leave.

Other people may also encourage you to take the blame for the abuse you've experienced.

Everybody is afraid of rape and sexual abuse. If your experience makes other people feel unsafe or out of control they may turn their fears on to you.

When these messages come from other people, they become even more powerful. Eventually the guilt grows into shame. And shame can be overwhelming.

All of this time you have been doing the best you can to look after yourself. But these ways of coping that made sense at the time can eventually become the thing that is holding you back.

I wish I could give you one of these.

5 EASY STEPS TO LIFELONG HAPPINESS AFTER SEXUAL ABUSE

Rebuilding a life after sexual abuse isn't easy or quick. But with hard work and support - it <u>can</u> be done.

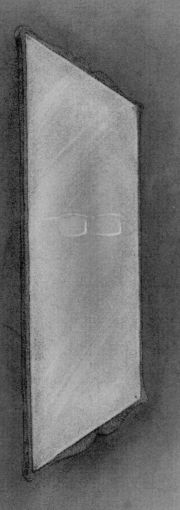

Chapter 3

I see me in you.

My past could overwhelm other people.
I WAS ABUSED.
I'm fine...
...see?
Often I would feel guilty and end up having to comfort them.

I found that it was possible to feel alone even if you have support.
I know you care...
...but you're not able to help me.

The women helped me to see the strength I hoped to have in future.
I did it - I told her that I could no longer do all of her cleaning.
I told her I needed more time for me.

...and recognise the painful places
that I had been in the past.

When their pain made me feel desperate and useless...
...I had a glimpse of how people who care about me must feel about my pain.

By feeling compassion for them...

...I was able to feel compassion for myself.

During my time in the group I had some difficult messages to hear.

I don't know if I would have been able to hear them if it wasn't for the other people who were at my side.

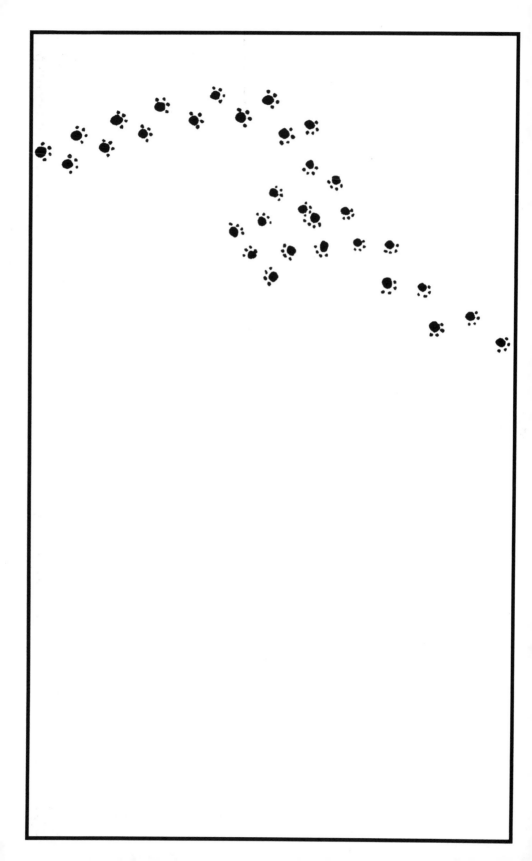

Chapter 4

Along came hope

I'd lived most of my life like **this.**

My life was small and lonely,

but I could control it.

Nothing happens here.

Then hope came along and I dared to wonder...

But hoping for a better life...

What a better life would be like.

wasn't easy

I had found a way of coping.
A way of containing my past.
Containing my Pain.

A better life would mean looking at my past—so that I can learn to live with it.

Taking control of where my life is going—

Instead of floating at sea.

GRAB

Letting my feelings out.

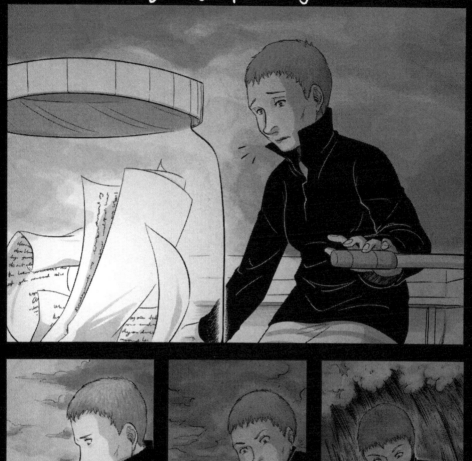

So that I can learn to **feel** again.

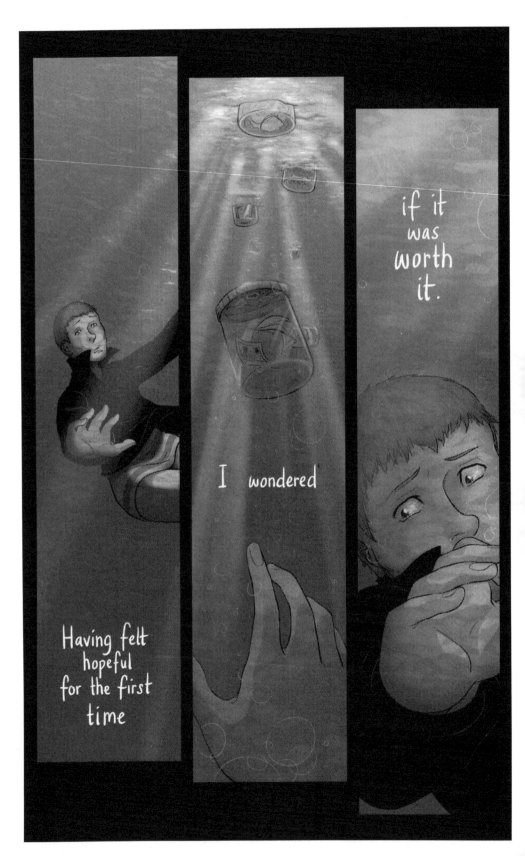

My life had been like this for so long.

How could I find the courage

to take those first steps?

My
journey
had
begun.

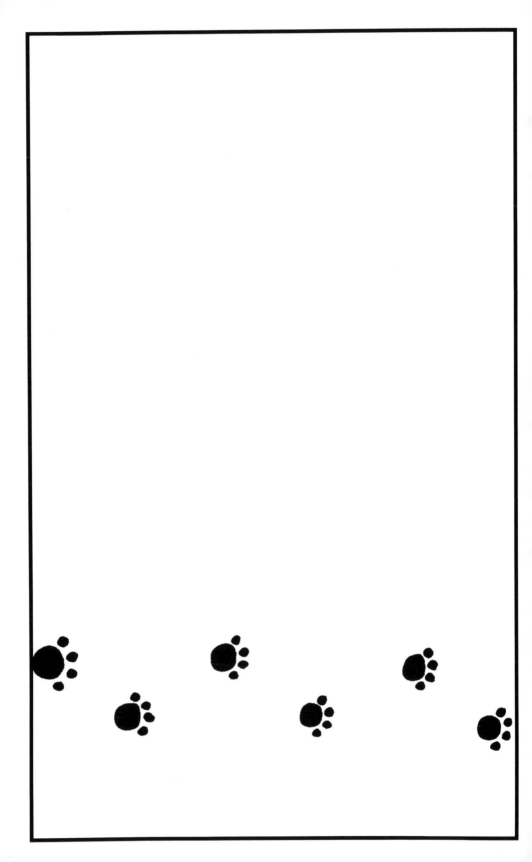

CHAPTER
FIVE

The Courage
to Be Me

But every journey is made up of single steps.

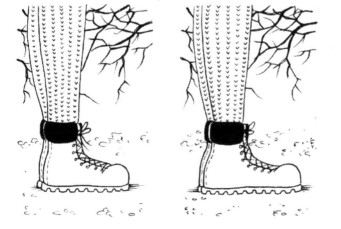
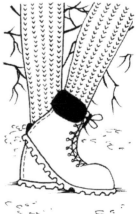

This journey is full of tough steps.

...and I know there will be more.

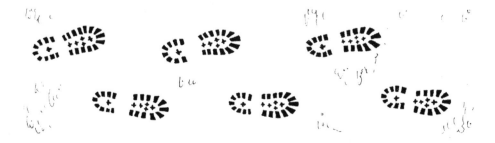

But meeting the other women here and learning what I've learned...

For a long time I tried to pretend that it didn't really happen.

I wasn't sure I was ready.

I always thought nobody would believe me.

... I can see
how much I've
grown already.

My real self.

And others have
seen it too.

It's like you're a new person.

I need to find compassion for the choices I have made in the past.

Choices to protect myself...

...to feel safe.

There are bound to be moments when I feel
like I need my old ways of coping again.

But there is more to me than my past.

I'm the woman who experienced something horrible...

...who still carries it with her.

But I want to be so much more than that.

I'm still growing into this woman.

She's the woman I hope to be.

I aspire to be.

I deserve
to be.

And I choose to be.

I feel like this journey is about
having the courage to come home.

I'm coming home
to myself.

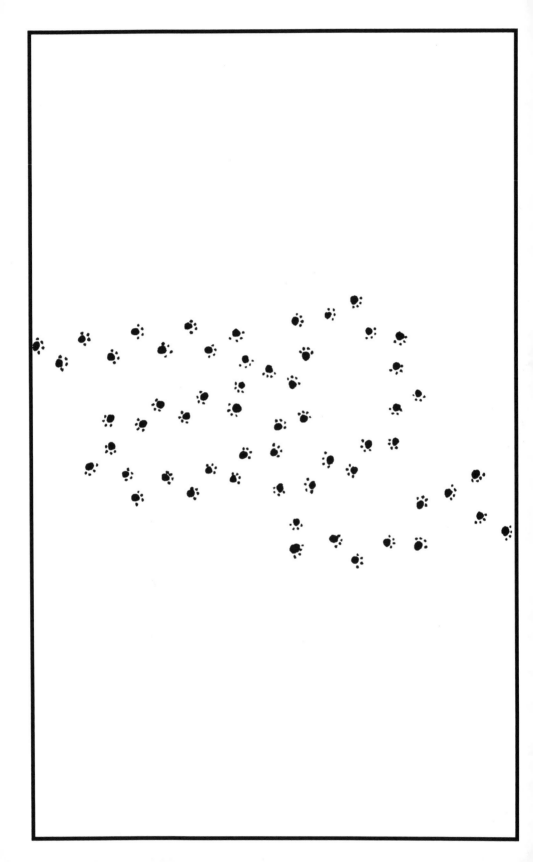

Chapter 6

This
one's
for
you.

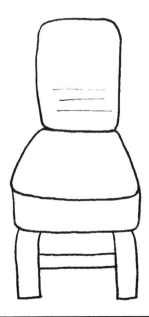

If this story has been your story there has always been a space here for you.

And there always will be.

Everyone is affected by rape or sexual abuse differently.

Some people are able to take great comfort from their faith, family, or pastimes.

But many people struggle.

And they struggle alone.

They tell themselves that they don't need help

Hmmm. Maybe if I leave it alone it'll grow back.

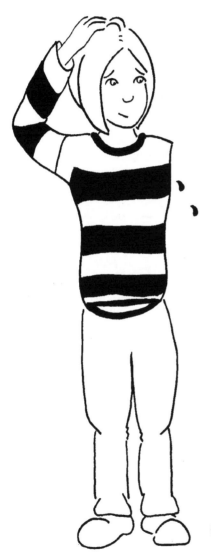

They tell themselves that they don't deserve help.

They worry that they may be beyond help.

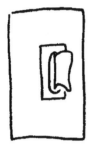

...and so that's what happened and that's how I feel about it.

Gulp! I'm going to get my supervisor.

At best they are living their life
in a holding pattern.

At worst they are living in crisis.

If this is you please know that...

Help *is* out there.

You *do* deserve it.

There *are* people who will listen.

There are people who will understand.

Just like the women in this book,
the steps you need to take will be tough.

...and you won't always
be successful.

You need to find the support that you deserve - this might take some time.

If you are struggling to find your courage
please know that:

And if you think that no one cares
please know that:

The illustrators of this book care.

The 106 people who helped to fund this book care. Including:

Ali Hodgson	Sara Wood
Caroline Schofield	Shuet Han Tsui
Cynthia Ellis	Wendy Mallas
Elle Lygate	John Hitchin
Rebecca Mitchell	Amanda Feldman
Kate Blewett	Sarah Clake
Judy Faulkner	Tessa Horvath
Kerry Evans	Fiona MacLeod
Muffin	Hollie Carr
Matt Killeen	Charlotte Hosier
Nicola Power	Victoria Lambert
The Friedman Family	Emily Burrowes
Roanne Dods	Hannah Berry
David Hayes	Inga Radziejewski

Andy Curtis
Heather Wilson
Sally Jane Thompson
Harri Sutherland-Kay
Jessica Cheeseman
Jacqui Farrants
Kyra Maya Phillips

Sarat Jones
Lucy Watt
Selina Lock
Laura Smith
Jody Day
Chris Packe
Kirsty Lowe

Chris and Joe Gill

Sally-Ann Smith

The Darvill family

Fumane Kokoali and Helen Keevy

Shirley Chiu and Dimple Devadas

Hayley Sudbury and Sheena Macrae

The Wragg family

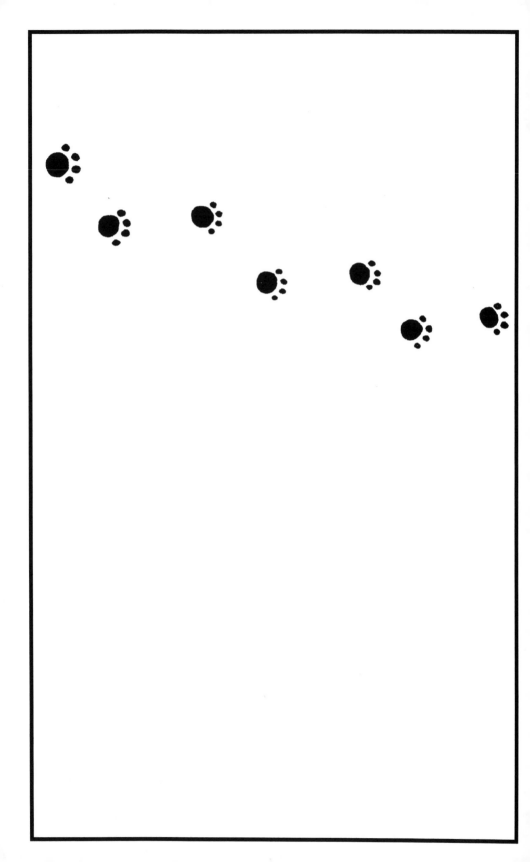

Epilogue
Kim's story

Kim sits with The Tears

The Toxic

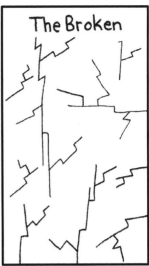

The Broken

She is someone who will Listen.

Understand

Question

Support

We should celebrate Kim.

We should thank her for doing something that most of us wouldn't feel able to do.

We should thank her for being an expert at what she does:

We should thank her for being there - in case someone we love needs her help.

Kim spends her time chasing funding.

Fighting to keep PARCS open.

Being the barrier between the charity and closure.

I don't want you to feel sorry for Kim, and neither does she.

I don't really like parades.

Kim doesn't want to be celebrated. She wants to be able to do her job.

Kim is not alone.

There are people like Kim throughout the country.

Doing good work – but fighting to keep their organisations alive. They could be even more brilliant. They want to be even more brilliant. But they need your help.

But the one thing that would make the biggest difference to Kim is a regular income.

A regular donation, no matter how small, will untie her hands.

And give her the freedom and the security to make PARCS even better.

Set up a standing order to:

PARCS

For the sum of:

£5.00 per month

CONFIRM

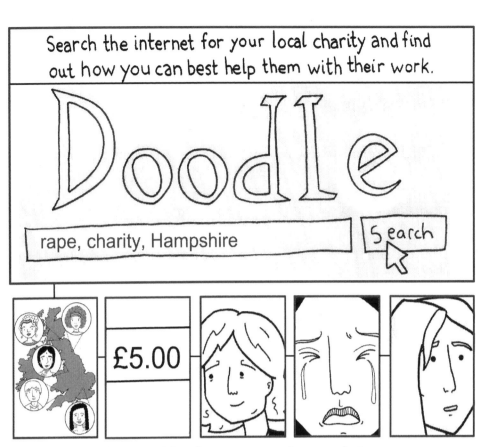

Search the internet for your local charity and find out how you can best help them with their work.

Doodle

rape, charity, Hampshire | Search

£5.00

People like Kim can only work to solve sexual abuse if you help them.

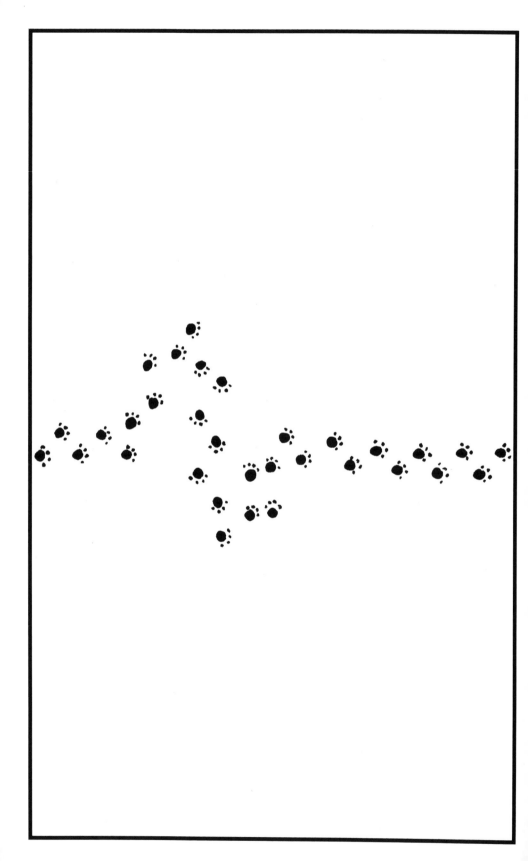

The illustrators

Alexander Bertram-Powell

Chapter 3

@alexbpart

www.alexbpart.com

Katie Green

Chapter 5

@katiegreenbean

www.katiegreen.co.uk

Jade Sarson

Chapters 1 & 4

@jadedlyco

www.teahermit.co.uk

Heather Wilson

Epilogue

@heatherjkwilson

www.missheather.co.uk

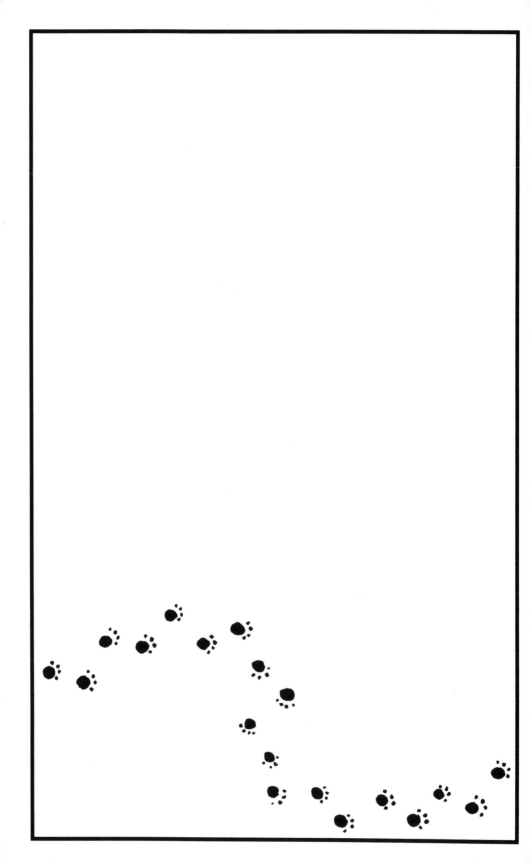

About the author

DR NINA BURROWES

Dr Nina Burrowes is a psychologist and researcher who specialises in the psychology of rape and sexual abuse.

Ha! I look nothing like that!

Dr Nina Burrowes is a psychologist and researcher who specialises in the psychology of rape and sexual abuse.

I originally began learning to draw as a way of relaxing from my day job.

Now I use my drawings to help people
understand the things they may
normally avoid...

VULNERABILITY

GUILT  DOUBT

ANXIETY

SHAME

...to celebrate the things about us humans that are brilliant...

AUTHENTICITY

LOVE

COURAGE

INTEGRITY

CREATIVITY

...and to tell the stories that don't normally get told.

Whilst I write about lots of different topics all of my work is about one thing:

I help people understand people.

Find out more at
www.ninaburrowes.com

The bit where it ends.

Thank you for reading
The courage to be me.

I hope it's helped you
learn more about life
after rape or sexual abuse.

I have written this book for the many people who are living with sexual abuse on their own.

I want these people to find my book.

But I can't do it on my own.

Please help people find this book.

Talk about it on social media.
Write a book review.

The end.

Other titles by Nina Burrowes

The little book on authenticity

Made in the USA
Columbia, SC
27 June 2018